Central Rockies
WILDFLOWERS

D0400504

A 'Pack-it' Pocket Guide

Central Rockies
WILDFLOWERS

LUMINOUS
COMPOSITIONS

Mike Potter

Text copyright © 1996 by Mike Potter.
Photographs copyright © 1996 by Mike Potter, Al Williams, Julie Hrapko, and Shirley Truscott.
Photographs by Mike Potter except as otherwise credited.

All rights reserved. No part of this book may be reproduced in any form without written permission from the publisher, except by a reviewer who may quote brief passages in a review.

Published by
Luminous Compositions
P.O. Box 2112, Banff, Alberta, Canada T0L 0C0

Canadian Cataloguing in Publication Data

Potter, Mike, 1954-
  Central Rockies Wildflowers

(A 'Pack-it' Pocket Guide)
Includes index.
ISBN 0-9694438-3-8

  1. Wild flowers–Rocky Mountains, Canadian (B.C. and Alta.)–Identification.
I.Title. II.Series.
QK203.R63P68 1996   582.13'09711   C96-900045-6

Printed on recycled paper and bound by
Quality Colour Press, Edmonton, Alberta, Canada

Front cover photograph: Alpine meadow near Bow Summit, Banff National Park.
Back cover photograph: Prickly Wild Rose *(Rosa acicularis)*.

Contents

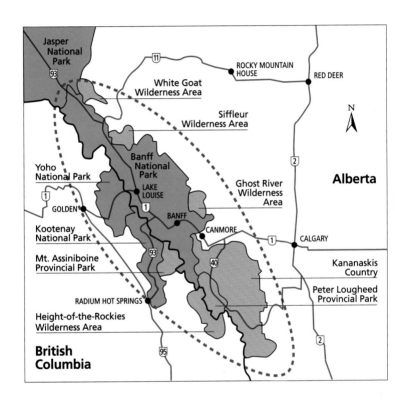

The **Central Rockies Ecosystem** is the area inside the blue dashed line.

Wildflowers are a highlight of many outdoor experiences, from peaceful strolls to energetic hikes. We luxuriate in the visual feast of bold colours; we breathe deep the sweet fragrances. Intrigued by these often delicate–yet at times amazingly hardy–creations, we wish to discover more.

Central Rockies Wildflowers is a guidebook to over 115 species of wildflowers in the Central Rockies Ecosystem (see map opposite and glossary, p. 81). This compact book describes, and illustrates with photographs, the most common wildflowers in the Central Rockies as well as quite a few of the more unusual ones. The aim is to encourage appreciation and understanding of this flora... at times simple, at times spectacular, always captivating.

Enjoying wildflowers: Al Williams photographing Western Wood Lilies.

The organization of species in this book is first by colour and then by flower shape. The four colour groupings are: blue & purple, red & pink, white & green, and yellow & orange. A colour bar runs across the page above each species description and accompanying photograph(s). The flower shapes vary: four petals , five petals , six petals , more than six petals , and irregular petals . The icon for the flower shape of each species sits within the colour bar.

This combination of colour and flower structure enables quick identification of the wildflowers.

The common name, as well as an alternate common name in many cases, and the scientific name of each species appear within the colour bar. The scientific name gives a conclusive reference to each wildflower since the Latin for genus and species is unique to a particular plant, whereas common names can vary.

The non-technical descriptions elaborate on the flower structure and leaf type. They also include additional features of particular inter-

Tenacity: River Beauty and Red Paintbrush near the toe of the Southeast Lyell Glacier, Banff National Park.

est, such as whether the species has a fragrance, the botanical family to which it belongs, and adaptations it has evolved.

The plants in this book range through elevation from low montane valleys to high above treelimit in the alpine zone. Some species occur across that whole spectrum. The variety of habitats that these wildflowers frequent is wide-ranging too, including prairie-like grasslands, wetlands, stands of deciduous trees, coniferous forests, open meadows, unstable scree slopes, and windswept tundra-like terrain. Again, one species may be found in a number of these different situations.

Because of this pronounced overlap, an indication of where to expect each plant is given in the species descriptions in *Central Rockies Wildflowers* (rather than attempting to gather them into arbitrary categories).

The flowering times of plants–even within one species–vary widely according to factors such as temperature, elevation, latitude, precipitation, and aspect (e.g., whether facing north or south). Due to this variation, this book does not attempt to indicate blossoming seasons for individual species. General reference to when you can expect a wildflower to be in bloom is often made, however, particularly if it is one that appears early in the wave of colours that the floral display presents.

Since no wildflower should be picked (definitely not in protected areas) and also because of space constraints, this book does not usually discuss edible or Native uses. It does mention if a species is poisonous.

This book covers species native to the Central Rockies, primarily those that are herbaceous: with the parts above ground dying back at the end of the growing season. It does include several widespread shrubs–with persistent woody stems–that are generally less than one metre (1 m) in height.

Illegal picking: Discarded wildflowers.

The scope of *Central Rockies*

Wildflowers does not encompass exotic (non-native) species, though some of them are widespread. So you'll not find descriptions here of plants like Common Dandelion, Goatsbeard, Bull Thistle, Common Mullein, Ox-eye Daisy, Butter-and-eggs, Bladder Campion, Heal-all, and Red Clover.

A glossary, with a general flower diagram, follows the species accounts on page 81. Next is an index of common names, and then an index of scientific names.

Wildflowers should never be picked. Wrenching a plant out of the soil destroys its life and denies others the pleasure of observing it in its proper setting. You should also be conscious of trampling on vegetation: keep to established trails where provided, and step carefully if you do travel off-trail.

Knowing more about wildflowers–learning to recognize individual species, discovering their fascinating features, becoming aware of their ecological significance–leads us to hold them in high esteem. As members of the plant kingdom, they perform the essential processes of photosynthesis: using solar energy to convert water, minerals, and carbon dioxide into carbohydrates for their requirements, while also releasing water vapour and free oxygen. This fundamental transformation, the basis for nearly all life on Earth, makes plants an irreplaceable part of the global ecosystem.

Coming to value wildflowers could lead you to support efforts to ensure their survival and maintain biodiversity. You can join a local natural history or botany group, or become a member of a regional or national conservation organization. By devoting energy to such a body, you will help to guarantee that we continue to enjoy the beauty of wildflowers and that they continue to fill their roles in Nature.

Ecological significance: A pollinating bee on a Heart-leaved Arnica.

Acknowledgements

I greatly appreciate the support given to this project by Robert Doull, President, WestMount Press Limited.

Special thanks to Jacob Reichbart for his generous efforts in the production of this book, including advice on design and pre-press.

I am grateful to Al Williams, Julie Hrapko, and Shirley Truscott for their excellent photographs.

Kudos to feather Mills for help with proofreading.

Anne Young made a helpful suggestion regarding the book's organization.

John Blum offered valuable pointers on book retailing.

Thanks to everyone who has shared their enthusiasm for wildflowers with me.

Dedicated to all who put energy toward protecting natural habitats.

Alpine Wallflower
Erysimum pallasii

Oddly named, Alpine Wallflower is anything but shy and retiring. Its purple blossoms stand out like a beacon on the rocky alpine slopes where it is found, while its fragrant odour is a sensory treat in an otherwise stark setting. The four petals in a cross shape, and the curved seedpods that form after pollination, confirm this as a member of the mustard family.

Purple Clematis
Clematis columbiana

Large coloured sepals (this species has no petals) draw attention to this, one of the few vines in the Rockies. The supple stems, with three-parted opposite leaves, trail and climb on other vegetation in the montane zone. A twisting mass of greyish styles follows blooming of the flowers of Purple Clematis, which belongs to the buttercup family.

Purple Saxifrage
Saxifraga oppositifolia

Ground-hugging clusters of this species eke out a living at high elevations, presenting rich hues in often austere surroundings. Tight rosettes of leaves grow close together, each bringing forth a short-stemmed flower. Especially considering its habitat, Purple Saxifrage blooms very early: soon after the winter snow melts.

Felwort, Four-parted Gentian
Gentiana propinqua

The lavender flowers of this member of the widespread gentian family vary according to habitat: numerous at lower elevations, single in the alpine zone (as illustrated). Higher situations also lead to shorter stems and fewer of the opposite leaves. The stems are often purplish. The fused petals of Felwort open slightly at top.

Al Williams

Common Harebell
Campanula rotundifolia

Fittingly, the lavender blossoms of this abundant and widespread species are bell-shaped. Usually hanging down or pointing sideways, Common Harebell flowers sit atop a thin, flexible stem. The oval or heart-shaped basal leaves soon wither, leaving narrow leaves ascending alternately up the stem. Contrary to its fragile appearance, this favourite wildflower is tenacious.

Alpine Harebell
Campanula lasiocarpa

This diminutive yet dashing cousin of Common Harebell occurs only above treeline. It grows on scree and stony areas, where the single flower appears oversize in relation to the tiny leaves. This strategy exhibited by Alpine Harebell is frequent above treelimit, where a large flower enhances the probability of pollination, while miniature leaves conserve energy.

Lungwort
Mertensia paniculata

These nodding blue flowers (pink in bud) are a marvelous bonus in damp habitats at all elevations. This bushy plant grows to over a metre in height. The multiple fuzzy stems of Lungwort have basal leaves with pronounced veining and long stalks; the alternate stem leaves are short-stalked to stalkless.

Jacob's Ladder
Polemonium pulcherrimum

The blue flowers of Jacob's Ladder are found from montane valleys to the alpine zone in open, well-drained locations. The multiple ladder-like basal leaflets account for the common name. The deep yellow centre of each blossom serves as a target for pollinating insects. This species, whose stems are reddish, belongs to the phlox family.

Alpine Forget-me-not
Myosotis alpestris

A charming and popular plant, Alpine Forget-me-not is a wild-flower whose discovery is always an uplifting experience. The blue buttons with yellow centres never fail to inspire, particularly growing as they do under rugged conditions. The highly perfumed flowers grow tight together at first, then elongate into one-sided spires.

Wild Blue Flax
Linum lewisii

The delicate beauty of this species is a fleeting thing, for each flower lasts one day only. The pale blue blossoms grow at the top of a tall slender stem with short linear alternate leaves. Wild Blue Flax (closely related to the flax cultivated for fibre, seeds, and oil) grows on dry slopes and in meadows, mainly in the montane zone.

Silky Scorpionweed
Phacelia sericea

A halo of bright stamens, with purple filaments and bold yellow anthers, surrounds the bottlebrush-like cluster of deep purple flowers of Silky Scorpionweed. Both the much dissected alternate leaves and the stem (up to 50 cm tall) show a garb of fine silvery hairs. This distinctive wildflower frequents open places, mainly rocky slopes in the alpine zone.

Blue Columbine
Aquilegia brevistyla

The flowers of Blue Columbine, with white petals and blue sepals, hang singly from the curved-over stem. Five blue spurs curl together at the top of the petals. The overall effect bears a resemblance to a group of doves perched in a circle, hence the common name (from the Latin for 'dove-like'). Not common, this plant with ferny alternate leaves—a member of the buttercup family—is found in open forests and meadows in the montane and subalpine zones.

17

These showy large purplish flowers with yellow stamens push up in early spring, a heart-warming sign of the return of above-freezing temperatures. The blossoms unfold before the leaves, often appearing with snow still on the ground. The common name Pasque Flower, suggesting its time of first blooming around Easter, is perhaps better used than the more frequent Prairie Crocus since this member of the buttercup family is not related to the crocus. Fuzzy white hairs garb the stem and deeply divided leaves. The luxuriant beauty of these wonderful wildflowers embellishes large expanses of montane grasslands and open forests. A tuft of feathery seed structures later replaces the flowers, catching the light on sunny summer days.

Blue-eyed Grass
Sisyrinchium montanum

The six flower parts of this species in the iris family are actually three petals and three similar sepals, each with a sharp tip. Each of the blue blossoms with yellow centre lasts but a day. The flattened stems bear up to five flowers each, accompanied by grass-like basal leaves. Blue-eyed Grass flourishes in damp open areas up to the lower subalpine zone.

Wild Chives
Allium schoenoprasum

Garden chives come from this species, which grows in open damp situations up to treelimit. The flower head of Wild Chives is a cluster of pale papery blossoms at the end of the stout stem. The accompanying round hollow leaves also sprout from an onion-like bulb. This plant belongs to the lily family.

Parry's Townsendia
Townsendia parryi

A large composite flower close to the ground, Parry's Townsendia blooms early in the season wherever it is found from the montane to the alpine zones. This species, with a blossom of yellow central disk flowers and a circle of violet ray flowers, favours open grassy or rocky sites. Short white hairs cover all green parts of this plant.

Sawwort
Saussurea nuda

This pioneer on stony ground is a pleasure to meet in its alpine habitat. Somewhat thistle-like, the purple disk flowers push out in a tight cluster from the short stem. Narrow, toothed, hairy leaves radiate from beneath. The pleasing odour of Sawwort is an unexpected surprise in such ascetic surroundings.

Kittentails
Besseya wyomingensis

An uncommon sight in open areas from montane to alpine elevations, Kittentails in bloom does look a bit like a fuzzy feline. The long stamens protrude from a purple flower that stands atop a short stem. Spade-shaped basal leaves on long stalks sprout from the ground, while shorter leaves attach directly to the stem. All green parts are hirsute, to employ the now seldom-used word for hairy.

Leafy Aster
Aster foliaceus

Aster species are numerous and highly variable, hence difficult to identify. Leafy Aster is a common representative of the genus, found in moist meadows and open forest at all elevations. Its blossoms, with their lavender rays and yellow disks, often grow in dense clusters. Asters are among the last wildflowers to bloom, giving a final hurrah of floral colour before winter sets in.

Common Butterwort
Pinguicula vulgaris

This plant is a meat eater… or at least insectivorous. Common Butterwort lives in wet situations where nitrogen and other elements are scarce, so to obtain important nutrients it digests small bugs that land on the slippery slopes of its slick (yes, buttery) light green basal leaves. The relatively large violet-like spurred flower apparently helps to attract prey. This plant occurs mainly at low elevations, and is always intriguing to chance upon.

Blue Beardtongue
Penstemon albertinus

The flowers of this species disport themselves in an elongated terminal cluster on the stem. The fused petals are deep blue with lavender at the base. The common name derives from the long yellow and white hairs inside the lower lip of the tube-shaped petals. Blue Beardtongue gets established on open, well-drained sites in the montane and subalpine zones.

Low Larkspur
Delphinium bicolor

This species–a shorter relative of Tall Larkspur *(D. glaucum)*–is found in meadows and on grassy slopes from low valleys to above treelimit. Each flower of Low Larkspur has a long spur behind the five blue sepals, which are larger than the petals at the centre. The leaves of this plant contains delphinine, an alkaloid that is highly toxic to humans. The buttercup family numbers this among its members.

Creeping Beardtongue
Penstemon ellipticus

A most pleasing flower, surprisingly large for its rugged habitat, Creeping Beardtongue frequents well-drained rocky subalpine and alpine slopes. The opposite leaves on this dwarf shrub may be deciduous, turning crimson before falling off with the frosts, or they may stay green through winter.

Wild Vetch
Vicia americana

This native pea is a common vine up to subalpine elevations, the purple flowers topping a riot of twisting tendrils. The opposite leaflets, up to 18 for each leaf, present a strong repeated pattern. The seeds of Wild Vetch, in pods that form by August, may be harmful to children.

Early Blue Violet
Viola adunca

This, the only violet in the Central Rockies that is actually primarily violet, bravely pokes up in early spring. Besides the attractive flowers, with their fringes, streaks, and spur, this species exudes a soothing perfume. The leaves are variable in appearance, though usually kidney- or heart-shaped. Early Blue Violet prefers low elevations, with habitats ranging from open and dry to shady and cool.

Silky Lupine
Lupinus sericeus

This eye-catching wildflower occurs in the southeast section of the Central Rockies, where its tall spikes of blue blossoms grace open areas. The distinctive leaves of Silky Lupine have five to nine parts, and are covered with fine hairs on both surfaces. Root nodes on this member of the pea family have bacteria that fix nitrogen, thereby increasing soil fertility.

Inflated red or purple seedpods (2-3 cm long) give this member of the pea family its common name. Preceding the seedpods are small purple flowers growing above finely hairy, much dissected leaves. Bladder Locoweed occurs in the alpine zone on bare rocky sites, where seedpods that break off when ripe are swept to new locations by the wind.

Showy Locoweed
Oxytropis splendens

This plant lives up to its common name: it is indeed attractive, the purple or blue flowers forming a terminal cluster above basal leaves with numerous finely hairy leaflets. Showy Locoweed, yet another legume (member of the pea family), bedecks open grasslands in the montane zone.

Julie Hrapko

Wild Mint
Mentha arvensis

Wild Mint, in common with other members of the mint family, features square stems, opposite leaves, and irregular flowers. The pointed leaves have serrated edges and minute glands on both surfaces. The sprays of purple or pink flowers grow in the upper leaf axils (the junctions with the stem). The fragrance of Wild Mint is renowned; Native people used its leaves to make tea. This plant is found in damp situations from low to middle elevations.

Julie Hrapko

27

Fireweed
Epilobium angustifolium

Very tall spires (up to 2 m) of these pink blossoms cover large areas in forests regenerating after fire. They also establish themselves on other disturbed ground such as slide paths and along roadsides. The long, narrow seedpods generate many seeds whose silky hairs aid wind dispersal. Fireweed, the floral emblem of the Yukon Territory, is widespread throughout the area of the Yellowstone to Yukon Biodiversity Strategy. The Central Rockies Ecosystem is a critical component of this visionary initiative.

River Beauty
Epilobium latifolium

The flowers of River Beauty are similar to those of Fireweed but larger and fewer in number. The height of this species is less than that of Fireweed. The leaves are alternate, like Fireweed, but shorter and of a bluer tint. A pioneering plant, River Beauty is especially abundant on river bars and streamside terraces–an inspiring example of tenacity under changing conditions. This plant is also referred to as Broad-leaved Willowherb.

Shooting Star
Dodecatheon pulchellum

The common name suggests a blaze of glory, and Shooting Star certainly adds a streak of colour to the meadows where it flourishes. The swept-back petals and dangling anthers create the impression of a pendant jewel. The brown cylindrical capsules that follow the nodding flowers straighten as they mature, helping to spread the seeds. This member of the primrose family is wide-ranging in elevation, with a preference for the montane zone.

Bird's-eye Primrose
Primula mistassinica

Once you recognize this tiny species, you will cherish it for its striking appearance. The single stem (only reaching 15 cm) from a small rosette of basal leaves supports a cluster of pink flowers. The deeply notched petals seem to spin round the yellow centre. Found in damp locations at lower elevations, Bird's-eye Primrose often grows in small colonies about a parent plant.

The red berries of ubiquitous Common Bearberry are indeed attractive to bears and other animals, though somewhat mealy to human taste. Native people used the berries to make pemmican, a staple food. The common name Kinnikinnik is a Native word translated as 'smoking mixture;' dried leaves of this species were mixed with tobacco. The tiny flowers display delicate shades and an unusual urn-like shape. The alternate leaves of Common Bearberry are evergreen, while those of Red Bearberry (*A. rubra*) are deciduous.

Prickly Wild Rose
Rosa acicularis

The popularity of this abundant shrub led to its proclamation as the floral emblem of Alberta, and to the license plate slogan 'Wild Rose Country.' Found in varied habitats, the large pink flowers of Prickly Wild Rose produce a fragrant perfume attractive to many insects and to human noses. Red rosehips form in autumn and can persist through winter, supporting a variety of wildlife. Hybrids do occur with the similar Common Wild Rose *(R. woodsii)*.

Moss Campion
Silene acaulis

This low cushion plant with many pink blossoms stands out brilliantly in the alpine zone, a welcome reward of reaching the land above the trees. The island-like growth form of Moss Campion protects it from desiccating wind, and collects wind-blown particles of earth and dead leaves to slowly build up soil. A deep taproot anchors the plant in often unstable ground and allows it to obtain water in what are usually quick-draining situations. Despite such adaptations enabling it to survive in harsh conditions, Moss Campion is a fragile creation that can take ten or more years to first flower.

Bog Laurel, Swamp Laurel
Kalmia polifolia

Found in wet places, as the common names indicate, this wild-flower features vivid pink flowers. An intriguing aspect of the ecology of this species is that the filaments curved inside the flower are under tension, and release when brushed by an insect. Pollen on the anthers thus settles on the visitor, which cross-fertilizes the next Bog Laurel it investigates.

Pink Mountain Heather
Phyllodoce empetriformis

Thick carpets of the bright bells of Pink Mountain Heather embroider sunny upper subalpine forests and open meadows above treelimit. The clusters of pink blossoms arch down from the tips of the short stems. The sepals at the top of each flower are reddish-brown. The evergreen leaves of species of this genus [see also Yellow Mountain Heather, with which Pink Mountain Heather hybridizes] are needle-like; compare the scale-like leaves of White Mountain Heather. The 'heathers' of the Central Rockies resemble but are not closely related to the true heather of Europe *(Calluna vulgaris)*.

Al Williams

Lapland Rosebay
Rhododendron lapponicum

Like many alpine species, this rare member of the Central Rockies flora blooms very early in the short growing season at its disposal. This adaptation is possible thanks to reserves built up in the previous year. The small evergreen leaves have a leathery texture that further enhances survival. Lapland Rosebay has a faint spicy fragrance.

Three-flowered Avens
Geum triflorum

This early-blooming member of the rose family requires sunshine and open spaces. The hairy red parts of the three flowers that hang above the finely divided alternate leaves are sepals; cream-coloured petals hide within. The stem of Three-flowered Avens is reddish; fine hairs cover the entire plant. Another common name for this species, Prairie Smoke, comes from the hazy appearance of the tufted fine plumes of the seedheads, particularly when backlit.

Windflower
Anemone multifida

The evocative name Windflower for this member of the buttercup family well suggests its open windswept habitat, from grassy montane slopes to alpine meadows. Lacking petals, Windflower has five or more brightly coloured sepals that present various hues. All other parts are hairy; the deeply divided leaves are mainly basal. The seedheads look like nothing so much as a thimble. The genus name derives from the Greek word for wind: '*anemos*.'

Twinflower
Linnaea borealis

The flared blossoms of this member of the honeysuckle family, two to a stem, emit a strong sweet scent seemingly out of proportion to their tiny size. The runners with their evergreen opposite leaves trace across the coniferous forest floor, often forming large carpets. The genus name of Twinflower honours Linnaeus, the Swedish originator of the system of scientific nomenclature. A famous illustration shows him with this, his favourite plant.

Nodding Onion
Allium cernuum

A member of the lily family, this plant has an onion-like bulb and grass-like leaves that release an onion-like smell when bruised. Nodding Onion is wide-ranging through the Central Rockies, found in open places from the lowest valleys to treelimit. A cluster of dry, upward-pointing capsules replaces the spray of dangling bell-shaped flowers.

Dewberry, Dwarf Raspberry
Rubus arcticus

Solitary pink flowers signal the presence of this low plant, whose small fruits *are* like raspberries. Dewberry, however, lacks the thorny stems of its larger relatives. The three-parted basal leaves are prominently veined and toothed. This species, a representative of the varied rose family, grows in wet places at all elevations.

Wild Bergamot, Horsemint
Monarda fistulosa

A jaunty representative of foothills flora, Wild Bergamot thrives on dry sunny slopes. It displays a large cluster of split petals surmounted by fused sepals and a spray of stamens and pistils. The square stem and opposite leaves mark Wild Bergamot as one of the mints; the scent it exudes also points to this affinity.

Northern Sweetvetch
Hedysarum boreale

Belonging to the pea family, Northern Sweetvetch has distinctive keeled flowers that lend their striking hues and fragrance to dry open sites at lower elevations. The string of pinched circular flat seedpods is an identifying feature of this species. Tiny silver hairs blanket the rows of multi-parted alternate leaves. The roots are an important part of the diet of grizzly bears, so be alert in the presence of this plant.

Elephanthead
Pedicularis groenlandica

No, we're not in Africa or Asia, there *are* elephants in the Rockies. An unusual inhabitant of marshy spots, Elephanthead on close inspection does indeed have curved 'trunk' and big 'ears.' The pink flowers group in a tight 'herd' on the tall stem, which–like the deeply divided alternate leaves–is often purple.

Bracted Lousewort
Pedicularis bracteosa

This distinctive plant, also known as Wood Betony, features a tall spike of tubular flowers atop a purplish stem. The curved blossoms are pinkish yellow and, as implied by the common name, are interspersed with bracts. The fernlike alternate leaflets do not appear until almost halfway up the stem. Bracted Lousewort favours moist habitats such as open forests and meadows in the subalpine and alpine zones.

Al Williams

Alpine Lousewort
Pedicularis arctica

Alpine Lousewort, with a short spike of pink flowers, is found only in windswept terrain above treelimit. The curved upper lip has two projecting tips, while the lower lip is three-lobed (the edges of the central lobe serrated). Hairy fuzz covers the stem and the fern-like leaves–a protective adaptation in its habitat exposed to high ultraviolet radiation.

Mountain Sorrel
Oxyria digyna

The inconspicuous green flowers of this member of the buckwheat family are much less noticeable than the later fruits, which are red papery circles around each seed. The dense basal clusters of long-stemmed, kidney-shaped leaves often turn reddish. Pikas, marmots, and caribou eat the leaves and stems. Restricted to the alpine zone but widely distributed through the Central Rockies and farther afield, Mountain Sorrel is usually found near water.

Julie Hrapko

Water Smartweed
Polygonum amphibium

As both the common and scientific names suggest, this is an aquatic or amphibious plant. Its glossy leaves float on the surface when it is growing in water. The numerous tiny pink flowers grow in a compact terminal cluster. A member of the buckwheat family, Water Smartweed is found in–or at the edge of–shallow depths at low elevations.

Red Paintbrush
Castilleja miniata

The paintbrushes are a conspicuous highlight of the Central Rockies Ecosystem, the range of colours of these species almost matching that of an artist's palette. Red Paintbrush is widespread, found in a range of habitats from montane valleys into the alpine zone. Pink flowers belong to Alpine Paintbrush *(C. rhexifolia);* there is also Yellow Paintbrush *(C. occidentalis).* One theory is that the differences in colour are due to varying amounts of trace elements in the soil. The bright parts that capture our attentions are actually bracts; the green tubes poking out between the bracts are the true petals.

The vibrant colours of this orchid match the image of dancing to lively music that comes to mind with its name. Pinkish sepals and petals spread above the lower lip, streaked with purple inside and splashed with gold–further embellished with purple dots–outside. The fragrant aroma of this sole member of its genus reinforces its tropical allure. Parallel veins mark the single oval-shaped basal leaf produced in the fall and persisting through winter, then dying after the flower appears. Calypso Orchids reveal their charm in shady forests–deciduous and coniferous–in early summer.

Four white petal-like bracts and strongly veined leaves identify this member of the dogwood family. (Though I have not seen this reported elsewhere, my observations indicate that plants with six leaves are fertile whereas those with four leaves are sterile.) At the centre of the whorl of leaves–which turn a beautiful burgundy in autumn–are the tiny greenish true flowers. These are later replaced by a bunch of berries: red and edible, though rather insipid. Bunchberry thrives on the floor of shady coniferous forest throughout the Central Rockies and indeed much of Canada.

White Mountain Heather
Cassiope mertensiana

The bell-like flowers of White Mountain Heather dangle from the tips of branches of tightly compressed leaves, issuing a visual clarion call in the upper subalpine and alpine zones. The reddish sepals contrast with the ivory blossoms on this plant, which grows in large mats. [The very similar Rocky Mountain White Heather (*C. tetragona*) has a deep groove in the leaves.] Though hardy to exist in its rugged habitat, this species has woody stems that are easily damaged, so avoid trampling on it.

Silver Rockcress, Fernleaf Candytuft
Smelowskia calycina

Clusters of small white flowers of this species can be abundant, though somewhat inconspicuous, on rocky high elevation slopes. The finely hairy leaves are an attractive blue-grey. Another, more colourful common name for Silver Rockcress is Fernleaf Candytuft. That this is a member of the mustard family is apparent from the four-petalled blossoms and long seedpods.

Northern Bedstraw
Galium boreale

The common name of this fragrant species refers to the former practise of using it to stuff mattresses. Sprays of tiny four-petalled flowers cluster atop the square stems. The narrow veined leaves grow in whorls of four around the stem. Northern Bedstraw is widespread, mainly in sunny montane forests.

Rock Jasmine
Androsace chamaejasme

Clusters of these tiny delightful, fragrant flowers bloom over a long period in varied open habitats from low elevations into the alpine zone. The tufts of Rock Jasmine spring at intervals from the horizontal stem. The compact basal rosette and short stem are replete with stiff hairs. The yellow 'eye' at the centre of the white petals seems to exert a mesmerizing influence if examined closely. This species, also called Sweet-flowered Androsace, fits in the primrose family.

44

Globeflower
Trollius albiflorus

The large showy blossoms of this species in the buttercup family appear very early, generally just as the winter snow recedes. There is usually a single flower, with five or more petal-like sepals and a green and yellow centre, atop each stem. The fresh green leaves are divided into five main lobes; the leaves on the stem are short-stalked to stalkless as they go upwards. Globeflower prefers wet meadows and streambanks, mainly in the alpine zone.

Western Anemone
Anemone occidentalis

Spreading their five or more veined petals wide, the yellow-centred flowers of Western Anemone bring an early spring burst of colour to damp subalpine and alpine meadows and clearings. The stems are heavily haired; the dark green leaves (which follow the blossoms) are very finely divided. The thick clump of feathery seedheads gives rise to the nicknames 'towhead babies,' 'moptops,' and colloquially 'hippies on a stick.' Western Anemone is a member of the buttercup family.

The five petals of this wild-flower have fine green veins and a delicate fringe along their lower edges. Five white fertile stamens radiate from the centre, alternating with five shorter yellow sterile ones. The bright green basal leaves have a curled-in shape; a single leaf clasps the stem roughly halfway up its 20 to 40 cm height. [Similar Alpine Grass-of-Parnassus *(P. kotzebuei)* is unfringed and lacks the stem leaf.] Fringed Grass-of-Parnassus often grows in clumps in damp situations from the montane zone to alpine heights.

Labrador Tea has wide distribution in the Central Rockies. Sprays of white flowers grow at the ends of the numerous reddish branches. The alternate leaves of this low shrub have curled edges and woolly undersurfaces–white in new growth, brown in old. Fading leaves turn bright red or yellow. Labrador Tea often holds sway over large areas in habitats with acidic soil, such as bogs and damp evergreen forests. Among the many uses by Native people and pioneer settlers was the brief steeping of leaves to make a hot 'tea' beverage.

47

Wild Strawberry
Fragaria virginiana

The pure white petals and yellow centres of Wild Strawberry bloom until late in the fall, though late flowering plants do not set fruit. The berry of this species is not as large as that of its cultivated cousin but every bit as tasty (including to the wildlife that help spread the seeds). The toothed basal leaflets occur in three's, with red trailing stems. This abundant member of the rose family is found at all elevations and in a range of habitats.

Partridgefoot
Luetkea pectinata

This diminutive member of the rose family forms extensive carpets thanks to creeping runners. The small white flowers are in a terminal cluster atop the reddish stem (to 15 cm high). The leaves, which grow both alternate up the stem and basally, divide often. Partridgefoot occurs in damp habitats near treelimit, primarily on the west side of the continental divide.

Shirley Truscott

48

Western Spring Beauty
Claytonia lanceolata

These small, delicate wildflowers signal warmer weather, first appearing just as winter's snow melts. The white blossoms have pink anthers and fine pinkish veins on the petals. The lance-shaped leaves grow in an opposite pair on the short stem. The corms are dug up to be eaten by grizzly bears and other mammals. Western Spring Beauty adds its subtle charm to moist meadows and slopes from low valleys up into the alpine zone.

Alpine Spring Beauty
Claytonia megarhiza

This rare beauty is a strictly alpine plant related to Western Spring Beauty. Its flowers are similar but the fleshy, spade-shaped leaves (often edged in red) are distinctive. The shiny dark green basal leaves have a waxy surface to cut down on moisture loss through evaporation. As the species name suggests, this plant has a thick, deep taproot (2 m or more long). These adaptations are essential for the survival of Alpine Spring Beauty in its habitat of open rocky places.

One-flowered Wintergreen
Moneses uniflora

As suggested by the species and common names, this wildflower has but one blossom per short stem (to 15 cm tall). The aptness of the alternative common name Single Delight is clear on turning up the nodding flower to reveal the pleasing pattern of 10 yellowish stamens and long protruding green pistil against the waxy white petals. The small, veined, rounded, slightly toothed leaves grow mainly in a basal rosette. The spherical brown fruiting capsule eventually points straight up. Fragrant One-flowered Wintergreen beckons on the shady floor of evergreen forests.

Al Williams

One-sided Wintergreen
Orthilia secunda

A line of tiny greenish-white, urn-shaped flowers dangling from an arching stem identifies this species. The pistil is distinctive: a knob-like stigma at the end of a long style protrudes beyond the petals. The finely toothed evergreen leaves are mostly in a basal cluster. You will find One-sided Wintergreen in shaded coniferous forests up as high as the upper subalpine zone.

Al Williams

50

Field Chickweed
Cerastium arvense

Deeply notched, veined petals are indicative of this species, which has narrow opposite leaves. The petals are two to three times as long as the five sepals. Field Chickweed favours dry locations in various habitats from montane valleys to the alpine zone, though mainly below treelimit.

Cliff Romanzoffia, Mist Maiden
Romanzoffia sitchensis

This unusual inhabitant of wet alpine crannies features small white flowers with yellow centres. The mainly basal leaves are round to kidney-shaped with shallowly lobed edges. The exotic-sounding name comes from Count Romanzoff (1754-1826), a Russian aristocrat who sponsored a botany expedition to the Pacific Northwest.

Spotted Saxifrage
Saxifraga bronchialis

Spotted Saxifrage is so named because of tiny red (sometimes yellow) dots on the small white petals–spots that are only apparent by looking closely. Another common name, Prickly Saxifrage, alludes to the basal cluster of sharp-pointed leaves. The numerous flowers of this species face the sun atop red stems up to 20 cm tall. Spotted Saxifrage, widespread in the subalpine and alpine zones in predominantly rocky habitats, often expands into large island-like mats.

Wedge-leaved Saxifrage
Saxifraga adscendens

This minuscule plant seldom reaches more than 15 cm in height, yet it makes up in fascination what it lacks in size. Green veins streak the white petals. The leaves, stem, and sepals all exhibit a glandular and hairy growth form. The tight rosette of basal leaves is often reddish in colour. The individual leaves display two shallow notches at the end. Wedge-leaved Saxifrage ekes out life in moist alpine habitats.

Shirley Truscott

Alpine Bistort, Viviparous Knotweed
Polygonum viviparum

This small member of the buckwheat family can be easily overlooked, its maximum stature hitting 25 cm. Tiny white flowers with protruding stamens crowd round the stem. The several dark, shiny basal leaves are lance-shaped, while the few stem leaves are in-conspicuous. Below the flowers are tiny bulbets that can drop off and mature into new plants, represent-ing an optional reproductive strate-gy. Alpine Bistort frequents meadows and damp locations, usually in the alpine zone.

Common Mitrewort
Mitella nuda

An outstanding aspect of this member of the saxifrage family, apparent on close examination, is the fine filigree of the petals. The five sepals and ten stamens, mean-while, come in standard shape. The delicate flowers grow in a series along the smooth stems, at the base of which lie the relatively large kid-ney-shaped leaves with toothed edges. Common Mitrewort is abundant in dense coniferous forests.

Julie Hrapko

White Geranium
Geranium richardsonii

The veined white flowers of White Geranium surmount striking deeply cleft opposite leaves. The word 'geranium' is Greek for crane; the term 'crane's-bill' is used for the fruiting capsules, in which the styles fuse into a beak-like pointed column. White Geranium occurs in trembling aspen stands in the montane and lower subalpine zones. Related Sticky Purple Geranium (*G. viscosissimum*) has glandular hairs on the stem, leaves, and base of each flower.

Valerian
Valeriana sitchensis

Al Williams

A dome-shaped terminal cluster of small flowers—pinkish at first, then becoming white—signals Valerian. Stamens and pistils protrude from the blossoms atop the square stem (to over 1 m tall). The veined opposite leaves exhibit a pattern of three to seven toothed lobes. There is an unpleasant odour associated with this plant, particularly after the first frost. Valerian prefers moist meadows in the upper subalpine zone, sometimes venturing above treelimit.

Twisted Stalk
Streptopus amplexifolius

    This plant in the lily family has, as the common name suggests, a zigzag stem. Small flowers with recurved petals dangle on thin kinked stalks beneath. The yellow-green blossoms take shade beneath ascending, alternate, veined leaves that clasp the stem (which grows up to 1 m tall). Red or orange berries follow as the seed-filled fruiting bodies. Twisted Stalk occurs in dense montane and subalpine woodlands.

Queen's Cup, Bluebead Lily
Clintonia uniflora

    Queen's Cup has an elegant flower of six white petals with yellow-tipped stamens. The usual solitary blossom crowns a short stem rising from two or three typically wide lily leaves. The common name Bluebead Lily refers to the shiny berry that follows. This species reigns over mossy haunts among conifers in the western part of the Central Rockies.

White Camas
Zygadenus elegans

The white blossoms of this species have green glands near the base of the petals. This member of the lily family has narrow, blue-green leaves and thin stems that support a spray of flowers. All parts of this plant can be poisonous. White Camas is common in dry open situations through all elevations.

Death Camas
Zygadenus venenosus

This close relative of White Camas is similar except for the fact that the smaller flowers are grouped in a tight cluster. It is even more toxic than White Camas. Death Camas, which blooms in early summer, occurs in grasslands and moist meadows at low to middle elevations.

Julie Hrapko

False Solomon's Seal
Smilacina racemosa

Zigzagging stems with large pointed leaves at each bend, finishing with a cluster of small spherical fragrant white flowers, distinguish False Solomon's Seal. Reddish berries, sometimes speckled with purple, follow at the end of summer. This member of the lily family grows in moist forests, for the most part in the montane zone.

False Hellebore
Veratrum viride

Very tall (up to 2 m) stems of this plant in the lily family carry long spikes of green flowers, later drooping in graceful tassels. The large, veined alternate leaves have accordion-like folds. This is a violently poisonous plant: to eat even a small portion results in loss of consciousness followed by death. False Hellebore prefers generally wet habitats in the subalpine zone.

Umbrella Plant
Eriogonum umbellatum

The flowers of this member of the buckwheat family appear as if made of thin paper. Mostly yellow-white with some pink tinges, they grow in umbrella-like clusters atop a stem up to 40 cm tall. Both the basal leaves and those at the top of the stem, just below the flowers, are covered with white hairs beneath. Umbrella Plant occurs from montane to alpine elevations in exposed habitats.

As the common name suggests, all parts of this plant (including the attractive berries) are poisonous. A terminal cluster of small white flowers caps the stem (up to 1 m tall) that rises above the veined, notched, toothed leaves. Shiny red or (less often) white fruits form in late summer. Baneberry, which belongs to the large buttercup family, dwells in shady, damp montane and subalpine woods.

59

Alpine Marsh Marigold
Caltha leptosepala

Yes, there are marshes even in the alpine zone, and this species is a typical resident of such spots. The dazzling white sepals of these flowers (which lack petals) contrast with dark glossy heart-shaped basal leaves. Yellow centres and a blue tinge on the underside of the blossoms add further splashes of colour to wet locations near and above treelimit. Alpine Marsh Marigold, which belongs to the buttercup family, grows to a height of some 30 cm.

White Mountain Avens
Dryas octopetala

Vast spreads of this hardy alpine inhabitant (a member of the rose family) enliven dry rocky habitats. The large eight-petalled white flowers have yellow centres. Both the leathery crinkled leaves and masses of feathery seedheads are reminiscent of Yellow Mountain Avens. Adaptations such as the ability to fix nitrogen, thanks to bacteria in nodules on the roots, contribute to the success of White Mountain Avens in colonizing rugged terrain. Its presence in turn stabilizes slopes and helps to build up soil.

Pearly Everlasting
Anaphalis margaritacea

Pearly Everlasting does not usually bloom before midsummer but the blossoms may persist until winter's first snow. White papery bracts surround the yellow disk flowers, on stems up to almost 1 m tall. The narrow alternate leaves, with a pronounced central vein, are white-woolly beneath. This species occurs in a range of open habitats at low to middle elevations.

Western Canada Violet
Viola canadensis

This enticing member of the violet family is white, with purple streaks on the lower three petals that serve to guide pollinators to nectar. A fringe of minute white hairs decorates the edges of the yellow centre. The large leaves are heart-shaped to oval, with wavy margins and strong veining. Western Canada Violet, which heralds spring, is often abundant in shady places at low elevations.

Sweet Coltsfoot
Petasites nivalis

This species is unusual in that the flowering stems emerge before the leaves. The flowers themselves are a perfumed cluster of white. The large basal leaves that eventually appear are strongly veined and deeply lobed; smaller leaves clasp the stem. Sweet Coltsfoot is common in damp situations in the sub-alpine and alpine zones.

Tall White Bog Orchid
Habenaria dilatata

This fragrant member of the orchid family presents spires of bright white flowers atop stems up to a metre in height. The narrow leaves taper in length as they reach up the stem. The genus of this species is also referred to as *Platanthera.* As the common name suggests, Tall White Bog Orchid prefers wet situations such as bogs and marshes, as well as stream and lake edges, at middle to high elevations.

Al Williams

Sparrow's-egg Lady's Slipper
Cypripedium passerinum

This member of the orchid family has the species name *passerinum,* meaning 'sparrow-like,' because of the resemblance of the purple-spotted pouch to a sparrow's egg. The terminal sepal arches like a hood over the inflated lower lip. The stem and leaves of this plant are all covered with fine silvery hairs. Sparrow's-egg Lady's Slipper evokes admiration in moist montane habitats such as streamsides and shady evergreen forests.

Round-leaved Orchid
Orchis rotundifolia

Mauve spots emblazon the white three-lobed lower lip of this attractive orchid. A pinkish hood arches over this distinctive feature, while two sepals point out to the sides. Three to eight flowers arrange themselves near the top of the stem (up to 25 cm high). As the common and species names indicate, the single large basal leaf is circular in shape. Round-leaved Orchid favours moist low elevation habitats, often in cool shady evergreen forests.

Double Bladder Pod
Physaria didymocarpa

Double Bladder Pod produces four-petalled yellow flowers at the end of stems protruding from a central rosette of pale green basal leaves. This member of the mustard family has a tenacious long taproot. Paired bulbous seedpods give rise to the common name. Few other plants grow in the vicinity of this species because it chooses completely open and sun-baked situations from montane valleys to the subalpine zone.

Yellow Draba, Yellow Whitlow-grass
Draba paysonii

Not drab at all (Draba actually comes from the Greek for 'acrid'), this plant explodes with colour in what we would consider unforgiving surroundings. Although it is small in size, you can't miss Yellow Draba bursting out in bloom among rocky places above treelimit. The members of this genus of the mustard family are difficult to identify, but all add subtly to our beautiful alpine flora.

Alpine Poppy
Papaver kluanensis

This uncommon native poppy gamely perseveres where few other wildflowers manage to gain hold. The five-lobed basal leaves are covered in pale hairs, while the oval buds sport dark hairs that absorb heat and help to hasten blooming. The seedpods of Alpine Poppy feature tiny openings that allow the seeds to be dispersed by the strong winds in its high rocky alpine habitat.

Yellow Columbine
Aquilegia flavescens

These graceful nodding flowers convey a sense of airy elegance with their flaring sepals, tubular and spurred petals, and dangling stamens. Sometimes tinged with pink, they hang from stems up to 1 m tall. A spray of finely divided, somewhat fern-like alternate leaves pushes up from the base of the plant. A member of the buttercup family, Yellow Columbine grows in a range of habitats from moist montane forests to alpine scree, but thrives best in subalpine meadows.

Stonecrop
Sedum lanceolatum

As suggested by the common name, this plant cultivates a preference for rocky places: the sharp-pointed yellow petals stand out in stony sites. The fleshy stem leaves often drop off before blooming; their red colour, heightened by sunlight, is most pronounced in exposed locations. Stonecrop grows through the range of elevations from montane to alpine.

Alpine Buttercup
Ranunculus eschscholtzii

Among the ever-popular native buttercups, this species is a bright addition to the land above the trees. The shiny yellow petals seem to reflect a glint from the sun and sky, while the deeply notched basal leaves have a dark green resonance. Alpine Buttercup will be met in moist habitats; the flowers reveal their glory in late spring and summer.

Alpine Cinquefoil
Potentilla nivea

The cheerful yellow flowers of Alpine Cinquefoil add colour to many a rocky slope above treelimit. The hairy silver-green leaves of this species are three-parted, unlike the Mountain Meadow Cinquefoil (*P. diversifolia*) of lower elevations, whose leaves are usually five-parted. [It thus conforms with the common name for this genus, which derives from the French *cinque feuilles* ('five leaves').] Alpine Cinquefoil–which, like other Potentilla's, is a member of the rose family–exhibits a cushion growth form.

Shrubby Cinquefoil
Potentilla fruticosa

This hardy, much-branched shrub (to about 1 m) with brilliant lemon flowers is well-nigh ubiquitous in the Central Rockies. The blossoms convey their points of bright through a long season from early June into October. Shrubby Cinquefoil presents alternate leaves (usually five-parted, though ranging from three to seven) and woody reddish-brown stems with peeling bark. This species belongs to the rose family.

Yellow Mountain Saxifrage
Saxifraga aizoides

Clumps of the tiny flowers of Yellow Mountain Saxifrage gleam in moist open areas up into the alpine zone, the yellow petals often spangled with minute orange dots. Narrow succulent (meaning fleshy rather than tasty in this context) leaves congregate round the short stems. Stout carpels (seed-bearing chambers), usually in pairs, later form at the centre of the five petals.

Yellow Mountain Heather
Phyllodoce glanduliflora

This species has small flowers almost closed at the end, in contrast with the open bell-like blossoms of Pink Mountain Heather and White Mountain Heather. The colour of the blossoms themselves is ivory; the yellow comes from the finely haired, sticky sepals and stems. The leaves appear akin to the needles of a conifer. Yellow Mountain Heather is frequently met near and above treelimit in damp situations. (Hybrids with Pink Mountain Heather may be encountered.)

Glacier Lily
Erythronium grandiflorum

Shirley Truscott

The swept-back petals of Glacier Lily grant it a dramatic air enhanced by the carpets of this wildflower that cover large areas from the montane zone to above treelimit in early spring. A welcome sign of warm weather, this display is an inspiring highlight of the floral calendar in the Central Rockies. The single, arched-over stem shoots up between two wide, tapering basal leaves. Both black and grizzly bears are fond of the corms where the plant stores energy for its brave push to the surface.

Oregon Grape
Berberis repens

The genus name of this species reminds one of the Berber people of northwestern Africa, which is appropriate since both share generally dry situations. The flower clusters produce blue berries that are indeed like grapes, though smaller. The shiny, leathery, toothed leaflets turn bright red in the fall. Oregon Grape is a creeping shrub found primarily at lower elevations.

Western Wood Lily
Lilium philadelphicum

The large, upward-facing, deep orange flowers of this lily can't be mistaken when in bloom during early summer. Dark reddish dots adorn the yellow area at the base of the petals. Narrow leaves grow in a whorl up the stem, which can reach up to 50 cm. This species occurs mostly in the montane zone, in habitats ranging from open grasslands to aspen forests. Thoughtless picking of Western Wood Lily (despite protected status) has greatly diminished its abundance and indeed threatens its survival.

Balsamroot
Balsamorhiza sagittata

The large yellow flowers of Balsamroot are found in western-slope montane grasslands of the Central Rockies Ecosystem. The large arrow-shaped silvery-green basal leaves have a fine fuzz on both surfaces. This species blooms in spring, bestowing a colourful aura to early season rambles. Mammals such as bighorn sheep, mule deer, and elk forage on this plant.

Wild Gaillardia
Gaillardia aristata

The large blossoms of Wild Gaillardia attract attention with their reddish-brown disk flowers and bright yellow ray flowers. This species, which blooms in midsummer, prefers dry montane grasslands. A grey-green fuzz covers the stem (up to 80 cm tall) and the variable alternate leaves that grow on it. This plant has the popular name Brown-eyed Susan.

Large-flowered False Dandelion
Agoseris glauca

The large yellow flowers of this species usually turn pink as they age and dry. This plant, though belonging to the composite family, lacks disk flowers. The basal leaves are not toothed or divided like those of true dandelions. [There is a similar Orange-flowered False Dandelion *(A. aurantiaca).*] Large-flowered False Dandelion occurs primarily in the montane zone in meadows and sunny forests.

Heart-leaved Arnica
Arnica cordifolia

The bold uplifting colour of its flower and its deeply cleft, opposite lower leaves make Heart-leaved Arnica a popular and readily recognized member of the Central Rockies flora. The wide ray flowers present a striking circle of yellow atop the stems (to 70 cm tall), each of which may have three blossoms. This species belonging to the huge composite family occurs mostly in glades in coniferous forest, occasionally reaching to treelimit.

Yellow Mountain Avens
Dryas drummondii

The nodding flowers of Yellow Mountain Avens often form islands of vegetation in rocky habitats. Nitrogen-fixing organisms on root nodules help this plant get a toehold in marginal conditions. Small, scallop-edged, dark green leaves with silvery undersides spread out in carpets 2 m or more across. The styles change into a tight twist of plumes that later opens into a silky sphere, the tiny seeds dispersing on the breeze. This hardy pioneering species in the rose family is best suited to low elevation valleys.

Golden Fleabane
Erigeron aureus

The small yet eye-catching blossoms of this plant are a delight to sight in the subalpine and alpine zones. The basal leaves and the mostly leafless stems are finely tufted. The common name fleabane originated with the belief in Europe that hanging dried bunches of species of this genus in a building would drive out fleas. Golden Fleabane is readily recognized as one of the many members of the composite family.

Alpine Hawksbeard, Dwarf Hawksbeard
Crepis nana

This member of the composite family may be little in size but it is big in hardiness. The small dandelion-like flowers grow in a compact cluster that pushes up from a long stabilizing taproot. A series of spade-shaped basal leaves radiate out from the centre of the plant. Alpine Hawksbeard scrabbles out its existence on scree and rocks in the austere heights above the trees.

Twining Honeysuckle
Lonicera dioica

The very fragrant flowers of this vine are yellow when they first bloom, turning reddish before falling. The leaves just beneath the trumpet-shaped blossoms fuse into a bowl-like shape. A cluster of red berries follows the flowers. Twining Honeysuckle is fairly common in low elevation forests.

This shrubby honeysuckle, usually about 1 m high, displays a pair of tubular flowers when in blossom. Even more attractive are the shiny black berries that replace them, strikingly highlighted by swept-back red bracts. These fruits are not palatable to humans but are on the menu of many animals. The large opposite leaves have pronounced veins. Bracted Honeysuckle occurs in moist shaded forests from montane elevations into the subalpine zone.

Yellow Paintbrush
Castilleja occidentalis

This is a creamy yellow relative of Red Paintbrush *(C. miniata)*, found primarily in subalpine and alpine meadows. Like most members of the genus, Yellow Paintbrush is parasitic, drawing nutrients from the roots of nearby plants. Don Domingo Castillejo was a Spanish botanist of the 1700s.

Flame-coloured Lousewort
Pedicularis flammea

The red tips and yellow lower parts of the flowers of this species do appear as if on fire, hence the common name. The purplish-red stems only reach a height of about 15 cm. The fern-like leaves of Flame-coloured Lousewort are much divided. Alpine terrain with a limestone base harbours this rare wildflower.

Julie Hrapko

78

Round-leaved Yellow Violet
Viola orbiculata

The yellow flowers of this violet have purple lines on the three lower petals. The circular basal leaves tend to stay green through winter. The small blossoms of this species, standing singly atop short stems, are a treat to discover in early spring. Round-leaved Yellow Violet is found in damp habitats from montane forests to the alpine zone.

Al Williams

Yellow Lady's Slipper
Cypripedium calceolus

This showy perfumed member of the orchid family never fails to elicit a gasp of admiration when spotted in its preferred habitat of damp low elevation situations. The shiny yellow lip has evolved into a slipper-like pouch with purplish spotting inside. The petals are brownish: the lateral ones usually twisted spirally, the upper one hooding the lip. Often growing in clumps, Yellow Lady's Slipper has conspicuously veined alternate leaves.

79

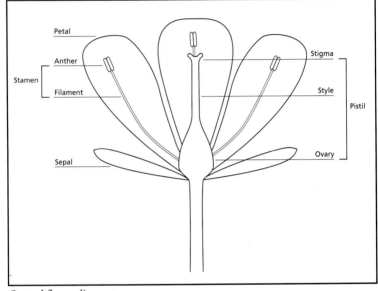

General flower diagram

Glossary

Alpine zone The land above the trees, in which only hardy plants grow [see treelimit].

Alternate leaves Growing singly from points on a stem; not opposite or whorled.

Anther The pollen-bearing part at the end of a stamen's filament.

Basal leaves Growing at the base of a plant.

Bract A modified leaf; distinct from a petal.

Central Rockies Ecosystem The area encompassing the foothills, front ranges, and main ranges between the Crown of the Continent Ecosystem to the south and the Greater Jasper Ecosystem to the north. It includes protected areas from Kananaskis Country in Alberta and Height-of-the-Rockies Wilderness Area in British Columbia north to Banff National Park in Alberta and Yoho National Park in B.C. [see map p. 6].

Composite A member of a large and complex family whose members have disk and ray flowers.

Coniferous Trees that reproduce by means of cones; conifers have needles (modified leaves) that are usually evergreen.

Corm A small underground bulb.

Deciduous With leaves that fall off before winter.

Disk flower One of the tubular central flowers of members of the composite family; distinct from a ray flower.

Family A group of related organisms, containing one or more genera, in the system of biological classification of all living things.

Filament The stalk of a stamen, at the end of which is an anther.

Fruit The seed-bearing part of a plant.

Genus (plural genera) A group within a family, containing one or more closely related species.

Habitat The particular area required for an organism, influenced for plants by factors such as temperature, humidity, wind, and soil.

Hybrid An organism resulting from cross-breeding of different species.

Lobe A division of a leaf, usually rounded.

Montane zone The low-elevation vegetation zone below the subalpine zone, above which trembling aspen does not grow.

Native An organism that occurs naturally in the area in question; not introduced from another area.

Opposite leaves Growing across from each other on a stem.

Ovary The floral structure in which the seeds develop.

Petal One of a group of floral structures in an inner ring, between sepals and stamens; usually white or a bright colour.

Pistil The female, seed-producing organ of a plant; consists of ovary, stigma, and style.

Pollen The male spores of a plant, produced by the anther.

Ray flower One of the strap-like outer flowers of members of the composite family; distinct from a disk flower.

Rosette A circular cluster of leaves, often basal.

Scree Small rock fragments below eroding cliffs.

Sepal One of a group of floral structures in an outer ring; usually green.

Shrub A plant, usually with multiple persistent woody stems, that is smaller than a tree (which usually has one main trunk and is over 5 m tall). [Even though they are technically not wildflowers, which die back to the ground each year, this book describes several shrubs since they look similar.]

Species An individual member of a genus.

Stamen The male, pollen-bearing organ of a plant; consists of a filament and an anther.

Stigma The pollen-receiving tip of the pistil.

Style The connecting part of the pistil between the ovary and the stigma.

Subalpine zone The vegetation zone between the montane and alpine zones, characterized by coniferous forests.

Toothed A leaf with numerous small notches along its edges.

Treelimit The elevation where trees become shrub-like; varies with latitude and aspect (the direction a slope faces).

Whorl Three or more leaves growing in a horizontal plane around a stem.

Further Reading

Bush, C. Dana, *The Compact Guide to Wildflowers of the Rockies*, 1990, Lone Pine Publishing, Edmonton. Intriguing ecological information, illustrations.

Cormack, R.G.H., *Wild Flowers of Alberta*, 1977, Hurtig Publishers, Edmonton. Comprehensive descriptions, photographs.

Gadd, Ben, *Handbook of the Canadian Rockies*, Second edition, 1995, Corax Press, Jasper. Excellent synopsis, illustrations.

Moss, E.H. and J.G. Packer, *The Flora of Alberta*, 1983, University of Toronto Press, Toronto. Technical reference, no flower images.

Petrie, Dr. W., *Guide to Orchids of North America*, 1981, Hancock House Publishers, North Vancouver, B.C. Fine treatment of this fascinating family, photographs.

Porsild, A.E. and Dagny Tande Lid, *Rocky Mountain Wild Flowers*, 1974, Canadian Museum of Nature, Ottawa. Brief notes on many species (with an alpine emphasis), illustrations.

Scotter, George W. and Hälle Flygare, *Wildflowers of the Canadian Rockies*, 1986, Hurtig Publishers, Edmonton. Good coverage of area, superb photographs.

Spellenberg, Richard, *National Audubon Society Field Guide to North American Wildflowers: Western Region*, 1979, Random House, Toronto. Wide geographic range, photographs.

Zwinger, Ann H. and Beatrice E. Willard, *Land Above the Trees*, 1972, Harper & Row, Publishers, New York. Fascinating study of the alpine zone, sketches and photographs.

Index of Common Names

Index of Scientific Names

The author at alpine meadows near remote Paradise Pass high above Lake Minnewanka, Banff National Park.

Mike Potter began working as a park interpreter in 1983, based in Banff National Park since 1986. Wildflowers are a central focus of his profession, including leading guided walks to renowned areas such as the Sunshine Meadows.

Mike's freelance articles appear in publications such as *The Globe and Mail*, *Nature Canada*, *Explore*, and *The Calgary Herald*. He is also the author of two trail guides, *Hiking Lake Louise* and *Backcountry Banff*, that include extensive natural history information.

Mike agrees with John Muir that "Everybody needs beauty as well as bread, places to play in and pray in where Nature may heal and cheer and give strength to body and soul alike."